KOALAS

LIVING WILD

Published by Creative Education

P.O. Box 227, Mankato, Minnesota 56002

Creative Education is an imprint of The Creative Company

Design and production by Mary Herrmann

Art direction by Rita Marshall

Printed in the United States of America

Photographs by Dreamstime (Buddhathakinga, Ongchangwei, Ppphotography, Robynmac), Getty Images (Altrendo Nature, Gary Bell, TORSTEN BLACKWOOD/AFP, Daniel J Cox, Gerry Ellis, Tim Graham, James Hager, Cameron Spencer, Time Life Pictures/Pix Inc./Time Life Pictures, Penny Tweedie, Norbert Wu, ZZSD), iStockphoto (Kitch Bain, Peggy Chen, Jeremy Edwards, Dan Fellow, Joe Gough, Matthew Jones, Ben Phillips, Amanda Rohde, Thorsten Rust, Smiley Joanne, Sawayasu Tsuji, Michael Willis)

Library of Congress Cataloging-in-Publication Data

Hanel, Rachael.

Koalas / by Rachael Hanel.

p. cm. — (Living wild)

Includes index.

ISBN 978-1-58341-655-6

1. Koalas—Juvenile literature. I. Title. II. Series.

QL737.M384H36 2008

599.2'5—dc22   2007008501

9 8 7 6 5 4 3 2

 CREATIVE EDUCATION

KOALAS

Rachael Hanel

The newborn koala inches his way toward the warm pouch on his mother's belly.

The newborn koala, which looks like a wet jellybean, inches his way toward the warm pouch on his mother's belly. He cannot see, and he does not have any fur, but he has strong senses of smell and touch. The **joey** relies on pure instinct to get where he needs to go. Once he reaches the pouch, he will stay in its safe darkness for seven months, growing bigger and stronger every day. When he is ready

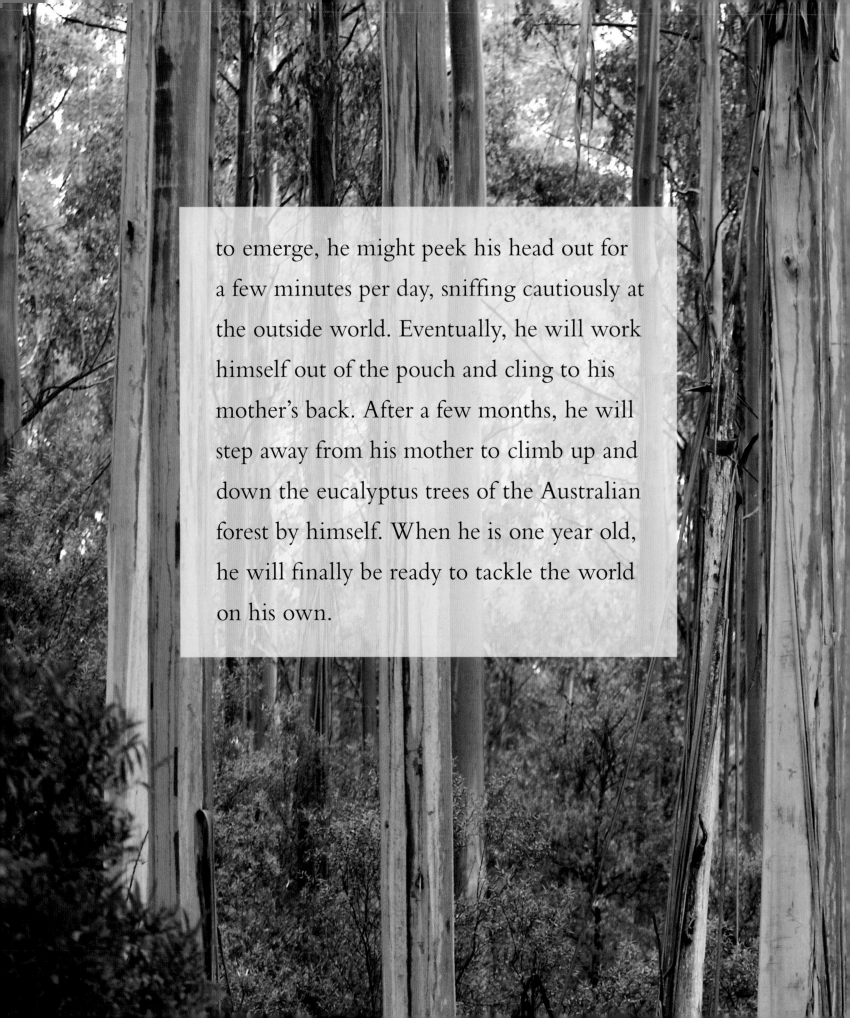

to emerge, he might peek his head out for a few minutes per day, sniffing cautiously at the outside world. Eventually, he will work himself out of the pouch and cling to his mother's back. After a few months, he will step away from his mother to climb up and down the eucalyptus trees of the Australian forest by himself. When he is one year old, he will finally be ready to tackle the world on his own.

WHERE IN THE WORLD THEY LIVE

Gray Koala
northern Australia

Brown Koala
southern Australia

Koalas are found only in Australia. Although gray koalas and brown koalas are the same species, they have different characteristics that enable them to survive in the different climate zones of Australia. Northern koalas typically have thick, gray fur, while southern koalas have long, brown fur.

THE BEAR THAT ISN'T

Wombats, like koalas, are herbivorous, eating mostly grasses and the inner bark of tree roots.

The koala is uniquely Australian. In no other part of the world will one find this furry, bright-eyed, tree-swinging creature. Its scientific name is *Phascolarctos cinereus*, which means "ash-colored, leather-pouched bear." Europeans who first arrived on the Australian continent in the 18th century thought koalas looked like little bears. Even today, it is common to hear the term "koala bear," even though that distinction is not correct.

The koala is a marsupial. Marsupials, such as kangaroos, have pouches on the fronts of their bodies where babies live when they are first born. In Australia, there are more than 170 types of marsupials. The closest relative to the koala in Australia is the wombat. Both the koala and wombat have pouches that open from the bottom, near their back legs, unlike the top-opening pocket pouch of the kangaroo.

The name "koala" first came from the native people of Australia, the Aborigines. The Aborigines also had other names for the animal, such as "koobor" and "colo." It is thought that the term "koala" means "no drink," because koalas do not need to drink water often.

Forty percent of Australia's forests have disappeared due to logging and clearing by people.

Koalas smell strongly of eucalyptus oil because of their diet; this scent also serves to repel fleas, ticks, and parasites.

Koalas are found only along the eastern coast of Australia, in the states of Queensland, New South Wales, Victoria, and South Australia. It is warm there, but not hot, with temperatures rarely rising above 86 °F (30 °C). Koalas live in the vast forests of eucalyptus trees. These trees are a koala's only food source, and each animal needs access to about 15 to 20 eucalyptus trees to survive.

There is no mistaking a koala for any other animal. Its physical features give it a distinct look. All of its body parts are built for life in the Australian forests. Koalas have round heads with alert, yellow-brown eyes. They are able to judge distances accurately, as koalas like to leap from tree branch to tree branch. Two ears with **tufts** of white fur are planted squarely on the sides of koalas' heads. Their big, flat noses look like black rubber spoons. Koalas have a strong sense of smell, which leads them to food and helps them find a mate.

The male and female koala look similar, except the female generally has a lighter-colored chest, and she has the pouch in front. The male koala has a darker spot on his chest, which is a scent gland used to mark his territory and attract females.

Koalas spend most of their time alone, eating eucalyptus or resting, preparing to eat more leaves.

Native to Australia and nearby islands, eucalyptus trees are also called gum or stringybark trees.

All koalas are covered with fluffy, gray-brown fur, which can make them appear much bigger than they actually are. Male koalas weigh between 25 and 30 pounds (11–14 kg), and females weigh slightly less. When on all fours, koalas are about two feet (60 cm) tall and three feet (90 cm) long from head to rump.

Koalas that live in the cooler areas of northern Australia sport a thicker coat than koalas in the warm, southern part of the continent. Northern koalas have short, gray fur that is densely packed together to retain heat. Two layers of fur help keep these koalas warm. They have a thick top coat with several hundred hairs per square inch (6.5 sq cm) and a layer of shorter fur underneath. These layers also serve as a koala's only protection in bad weather. Koalas do not make or look for physical shelter but find as much protection as they can in trees. During heavy rains and strong winds, koalas curl up so that their backs bear the brunt of the wind and rain. The fur on their bellies is thinner and not suited to being exposed to the elements.

Southern koalas have long, brown fur that moves with the breeze and allows for more air circulation. These koalas are also a bit larger than their northern

The longhaired koalas of southern Australia keep cool when breezes blow and ruffle their coats.

Koalas are good and fearless climbers, going to great lengths to get to the best spot in a tree.

counterparts. Koalas do not sweat, so to stay cool, they will lick their forearms. They also sit high up in trees and "fan" their limbs by dangling them off branches and letting them sway in the breeze.

The koala appears cuddly, but it is surprisingly strong. It is an expert climber, as it must scramble up trees to reach its food, the eucalyptus leaf. On the ground, a koala can run as quickly as a rabbit. Its two front legs are thin

and lean, while its two back legs are short and muscular. With its front legs, a koala hugs a tree trunk and then pushes up with its powerful back legs. In this manner, koalas can scoot up a tree trunk five inches (13 cm) per push. When they need to climb back down, they do so backwards, with feet and backside going down first.

The front limbs of a koala are known as hands, and the back limbs are called legs. A koala's hands are not like

On the ground, a koala can run at speeds of 25 miles (40 km) per hour.

Koalas are one of the few animals that have fingerprints. The fingerprints of humans and koalas share many characteristics.

a human's; they have three fingers and two thumbs with which they can easily grasp branches and leaves. On the feet, only one of the five toes acts as a thumb. The second and third **digits** are fused together, and the koala uses these digits to groom itself. The pads on its hands and feet are rough, which helps the koala to climb and also serves as protection when it leaps from branch to branch or from branch to ground.

A koala moves gracefully around the forest, all the while showing off its amazing flexibility. It can swing from branches or hold on to a branch with three legs while reaching around its body with the fourth. It can even hold on to a branch with just one foot and hang upside down. It shows a remarkable sense of balance, scampering across tree limbs like a gymnast on a balance beam. If a koala falls out of a tree, it has enough padding on its body to avoid injury most of the time.

Often, koalas do not travel more than a few miles from their birthplace during their entire lives, which can extend up to 17 years. The only exceptions are when koalas are forced to move, whether it is from forest fires, droughts, or human destruction of their habitats.

A koala's hands and feet are made for grasping things like branches and leaves and for climbing trees.

Koalas enjoy eating leathery eucalyptus leaves, even though the leaves don't provide much energy.

A LIFE OF LEISURE

A sleeping koala is a common sight.

Watching a koala for long periods of time, day after day, could become rather tedious. The animal's daily routine consists of just two activities: slowly munching on leaves and branches, and sleeping. A koala loves to sleep and dozes for 16 to 19 hours each day. It is a nocturnal creature, which means it moves around mostly at night.

Its diet, too, rarely varies. A koala eats only leaves and branches from the eucalyptus tree. Eucalyptus oil smells like a menthol cough drop, and the oil is often used in different medicines. That scent seeps through the koala, so the animal, too, tends to smell like a cough drop all of the time.

There are between 600 and 800 species of eucalyptus in Australia. The koala eats from only about 50 of the species, though, because some varieties of the eucalyptus tree are poisonous. Even a tree from which a koala ate in one month can change its physical makeup and turn poisonous the next. A koala possesses a strong sense of smell and can detect when a tree has turned poisonous just by sniffing a leaf.

Sometimes koalas supplement their diet. Besides eucalyptus leaves, they have also been known to occasionally eat mistletoe and box leaves.

Koalas do drink water, but not a lot of it. Eucalyptus leaves, which are about two-thirds water, provide the koala with plenty of liquid.

Koalas munch on one to three pounds (.45–1.3 kg) of leaves per day. They have these trees all to themselves; no other animal feeds from the eucalyptus tree. To eat, the koala grabs on to a branch with its hands and brings the leaves to its mouth. Its cheeks are flexible, so it can store leaves there until it is ready to eat them. A koala uses its **incisors**, **canines**, and **molars** to grind up leaves and make them easier to swallow.

Eucalyptus leaves are not the easiest to digest, but a specially designed digestive system allows the koala to break down its food. As food travels from the stomach, it passes through the intestine and sits in a storage area, called the caecum, until the body is ready to break it down, digest it, and turn it into fuel. Koalas do not gain much energy from this limited diet. This is why they move slowly, eat a lot, and sleep so often.

Koalas are more active during the breeding season, which occurs from September to January (summertime in Australia). The mating period is one of the only times in which koalas come together; otherwise, they prefer to live on their own. When males are ready to mate, they leave their scent on trees, using the gland on their chests. They also bellow loudly to let females know they are near. The deep noise sounds like the grunt of a pig or a thunderous human snore. Often, young male koalas are scared off by the sounds of a more dominant male. Young koalas must search for a space that is not already taken by another male. A female koala will also bellow, but her trembling call tends to be higher-pitched and is not heard as frequently as a male's.

Males start breeding around the age of two, while females breed when they are three or four years old. Females can produce offspring once every year if they are healthy and if their habitat is ideal and well-stocked with food. In less than ideal conditions, a female might give birth only once every two or three years.

A joey is born 35 days after mating occurs. But then it will live in its mother's safe, warm pouch for six to seven months. In the pouch, the joey drinks its mother's milk to grow strong. Koalas generally give birth to just one joey at a time; the birth of twins is rare. When the joey first emerges from the pouch, it eats a slimy, green substance called pap left by its mother. This discharge is rich in nutrients and helps strengthen the joey's digestive system when it is ready to eat eucalyptus leaves.

Even after a joey emerges from the pouch, young koalas remain close to their mothers for a time.

When the joey is ready to explore the outside world, it will travel only as far as its mother's legs at first, reluctant to leave its safe zone. But eventually, it will crawl onto the mother's back; this is her favorite means of carrying her joey. After a while, it will tentatively step away from its mother and nervously walk on a tree's branches. It might fall a few times or get scared, but it can always return quickly to its mother. Slowly, it gains confidence and spends more and more time away from its mother. Koala babies stay with their mothers for about a year, until they can live on their own. Then they wander away to find their own territory and prepare to start their own families. Although some female koalas can live as long as 17 years, the normal life expectancy of a male koala is 2 to 10 years in the wild and 12 to 14 years in captivity.

Some of the greatest threats koalas face come from nature. Wildfires destroy the natural forest habitat of the koala, forcing the animal to flee and find a new place to live. Drought can also destroy trees and force koalas to other areas to find healthy eucalyptus trees. Koalas are also susceptible to a parasitic disease called chlamydia. This can cause blindness and make females unable to have babies.

Once a joey (opposite) lets go of its mother and starts to climb, it can fall easily (above).

After mating, a male koala will have no part in raising his offspring and probably will never even see the joey.

Large tropical snakes such as pythons have no problems reaching koalas that are hiding in trees.

Koalas also face dangers from other Australian animals. A koala is usually safest in its tree; that is why it spends most of its day high up from the ground. On the ground, predators such as wild dogs, called dingoes, can attack koalas. Snakes, owls, and **goannas** are also threats. However, these predators usually prey on young or sick koalas. A healthy adult koala uses its agility to quickly sprint away, or it uses its claws to defend itself.

Koalas are defenseless, however, when it comes to human dangers. Many koalas die every year after being hit by cars. Humans live in close proximity to koalas, and many roads lead through the forests that koalas call home. A koala scampering across a highway often finds itself in the path of an oncoming vehicle. Roads throughout eastern Australia are peppered with signs alerting motorists to the presence of koalas.

Aborigines do not pose
a big threat to koalas,
but dingoes (opposite)
can be dangerous
predators.

A TROUBLED HISTORY

Koalas have been important to the native, or Aboriginal, people of Australia for the millennia that both have shared the continent. Aborigines once probably ate koala meat but did not regard it as a favorite food. Therefore, any koala hunting done by the Aborigines did not negatively affect the animal's overall population.

When Europeans first settled in Australia in the late 18th century, they took note of the curious creature and hunted it in small numbers. The first recorded mention of a koala occurred in 1798, and Europeans thought the animal was some type of bear or wombat. As more Europeans settled in Australia, they cleared eucalyptus forests to make way for homes, towns, and farms. Koalas started to move around more in order to find new habitats.

Not until another century had passed, around 1880, did humans start hunting koalas in greater numbers. European settlers discovered that koala fur was very warm when made into clothing and blankets, and demand for the fur increased around the world. Hunters also found that koalas were easy to capture and kill because

People who live near koala habitats are discouraged from letting their dogs run loose, which helps to prevent attacks on koalas.

Herbert Hoover served as the 31st U.S. president from 1929 to 1933.

When Europeans first observed the slow and sleepy-looking koalas, they thought eucalyptus leaves contained some type of drug.

they were relatively slow and seemed to have no fear of humans. Koala hunting would continue unchecked for 50 years, pushing the animal to the brink of extinction.

The koala fur trade grew rapidly. In one year, more than two million koala skins were shipped to Alaska alone. Koalas started to disappear from the Australian landscape, especially in parts of southern Australia. In northern states, their numbers plummeted to just a few hundred. Overall, by the early 20th century, there were only a few thousand koalas left, where at one time there had been millions. By the 1920s, Australians finally realized these animals could be extinct in a few years if hunting was left unchecked, and many begged the government to outlaw the hunting of their beloved animals. This type of public outpouring of support for an animal had never before been seen in Australia. People from all types of organizations—community groups, churches, schools, businesses, and women's clubs—joined together in protest.

The public persuaded the government to pass laws against koala hunting. But these laws were not always enforced, and the government often gave in to pressure

from fur hunters. But in 1927, future United States president Herbert Hoover, as U.S. secretary of commerce, signed an order that prohibited the importation of koala skins to the U.S. Hoover had worked for a time in the gold mines of Australia, so he knew how important the animals were to Australians.

The Australian government declared koalas a protected species in the 1930s. Still, there were isolated incidents of

Peaceful koalas, hunted in the first half of the 20th century for their fur, faced extinction.

It is estimated that 80 percent of the koala's historic natural habitat has been destroyed since European settlement began.

koala hunting by **poachers**. Also, the government did not protect the koala's food source, the eucalyptus tree. Even today, trees are routinely cut down as the land is cleared, leaving koalas in danger of starvation.

There are about 100,000 koalas in Australia today, numbers still far below their pre-hunting population. The status of the koala ranges from "common" to "rare," depending on the geographic region of Australia. For example, in the state of Queensland, the koala is considered to be common, except in the southeast portion of the state, where it is listed as vulnerable. In South Australia, where the koala was re-introduced in the 1920s after the fur trade had completely wiped out the original population, it is now considered rare.

Until 1980, the Australian government banned exportation of live koalas. The only place in the world that people could see koalas outside Australia was the San Diego Zoo, which has housed koalas since 1915. The San Diego Zoo was the only zoo that had figured out how to successfully keep koalas in captivity. A koala requires a particular habitat with carefully regulated temperatures to stay comfortable. Most importantly, zoos that have koalas need to grow many eucalyptus trees in order to satisfy a koala's appetite. With improved technology and greater knowledge, koalas are today found in zoos around the world.

Because of its cuddly appearance, the koala quickly grew popular with children and adults in Australia and throughout the world in the 1900s. When Australians protested koala hunting in the 1920s, many images emerged that compared koalas to children or showed them as being part of the family. Indeed, koalas can wrap their arms and legs around people and give "hugs," and they can also cry like human babies when injured.

The cute images of koalas easily transferred to cartoons. One of the first cartoon koalas to appear was Bunyip Bluegum, drawn by famous Australian artist Norman Lindsay in the 1918 classic children's tale, *The Magic Pudding*. In 1933, another cartoon koala, Dorothy Wall's Blinky Bill, appeared on the scene. Both Bunyip Bluegum and Blinky Bill helped endear the koala to Australians. Soon, koala cartoons would be found in all parts of the world. *Adventures of the Little Koala* was a cartoon that first aired in Japan in 1987 but later found a home on the

Today, zoos often offer the safest environment in which young koalas can learn skills and survive.

Coin collectors who are fond of koalas treasure images of the animal such as this.

It is illegal to keep koalas as pets, although in 1937, a woman from the state of Victoria took in an orphaned koala and named him Edward.

Nickelodeon television network in the U.S. Today, children in Australia and the U.S. can watch *The Koala Brothers*, an animated show that takes place in the **outback**. The koala brothers, Frank and Buster, have many friends and fly around the country in a little two-seater plane.

Perhaps the best-known koala **icon** is Teddy, the "spokes-koala" for the Australian airline Qantas. Teddy, a koala from the San Diego Zoo, began starring in Qantas commercials in 1967. In the advertisements, Teddy appeared grumpy because Qantas was able to fly people quickly and cheaply to Australia, and Teddy would have preferred to have the continent all to himself. The commercials made it appear that Teddy was talking and making gestures, which gave him a human-like appearance to which people could relate.

Because the animals are found only in Australia, koalas became a symbol of everything Australian, representing the "common man" and the tough spirits of Australians. Along with the kangaroo, Australians have adopted the koala as a national symbol, much like the U.S. has the bald eagle.

The flexible koala can sleep in almost any position but keeps its body rolled into a tight ball.

KOALA BE

What do those tawny wet round circles see . . .
Climbing ever climbing toward the blue?

The way you collect with lips so nimble,
Leafy spears that line the paths to heaven

But are they there? —and do you care? . . .
Chewing ever chewing minty breathed

You gaze out of a sleep more rite than waking
And mirror nightly the swirling arcs of stars

When if your tree springs the shapes of eternity
Would the stare of a 'supial bear witness more or less?

Would these claws grip any tighter?
Would the moon be any brighter? . . .

Cling little tuft, the echoing eyes are thing enough
Behind eucalyptus dreaming, the greenest sweet

Beating time the breast of miracles in branches sway
Splintering the sun blinks in the pouch of the universe

Mark Washburn (b. 1960)

BOUNCING BACK

Scientists still have much they want to learn about koalas' habitats and diets. Today, the bear-like animals are popular not only in Australia but around the world. Many organizations and individuals are dedicated to learning more about koalas in order to protect them and help their numbers increase.

More than 45 million years ago, the continents of South America, Antarctica, and Australia were joined together. Scientists believe an early form of koala traveled from South America, crossed Antarctica, and settled in Australia. About 40 million years ago, koalas and wombats are believed to have branched off from a common ancestor. Fossils of koalas have been found in western and southern Australia, places where koalas do not live today, but back then, Australia was likely composed of widespread rainforests. Some koala fossils, estimated to be 40,000 years old, are twice the size of today's koalas. These large-bodied animals may have become extinct when the rainforests disappeared and new trees could no longer support their weight. A dozen different types of koalas may have existed throughout the

Marsupials are common throughout Australia, but the only marsupial that is found in North America is the opossum.

Eucalyptus trees are cut down into logs for people to use as fuel and as materials for building things.

ages, but now only one species remains. Today's koala is believed to have been around for four million years.

Scientists and volunteers continue to study koalas today. Even schoolchildren help in activities, such as koala counts, to help researchers find out more about the animal. Each year, dozens of researchers and scientists, mostly from Australian universities, take on separate projects to learn more about the koala.

Common studies conducted by scientists focus on the koala's diet, habitat, and population. To track populations, scientists briefly capture koalas and put a band on their leg or a tag on their ear that contains a tracking device. This way, researchers can count exact numbers and be alerted immediately if numbers start to go down. Scientists also use taped mating calls to attract koalas out into the open, where they can be counted more easily.

To learn more about baby koalas, a recent study examined the pouches of koalas. A koala's pouch is sometimes dirty and lined with a crusty substance. But in studying female koalas during breeding season, researchers discovered the pouches contained a clean, clear liquid. By examining the liquid, scientists learned it contains

antibacterial components that keep pouches germ-free and koala babies healthy.

By studying eucalyptus trees, scientists can learn what makes certain ones toxic to koalas. Then, studying what the koalas eat and what they do not eat, researchers can determine what makes an ideal koala habitat and what their exact food requirements are. That information can be used when creating artificial koala habitats in zoos or when repairing old ones in the wild that have been destroyed by fire, drought, or **deforestation**.

Today, the koala still faces many threats, both in nature and from humans. But when natural disasters strike, humans are often there to help. In early 2007, Australia faced one of its worst forest fires in years when huge swaths of trees in Framlingham Forest, in the state of Victoria, were destroyed. Rescuers searched the forest for koalas that were burned or starving. Many were nursed back to health and released into other forests. The fires destroyed many young eucalyptus trees that had just been planted, so it may take years before koalas can return to the region.

In many parts of the world, humans **encroach** upon wildlife populations. More and more people like to live

Koalas prefer to spend most of their time in trees, where they feel safe. If they are forced to swim, though, they can do so easily.

Forest fires are a natural part of life for trees, but they disrupt the habitats of many animals.

as close to nature as possible, but such places are home to animals that may be negatively affected by development. This is the case in Australia, where destruction of habitat remains the biggest threat to the koala. The koala itself is protected, but laws regarding a koala's habitat are not always strongly enforced. Eucalyptus forests are routinely cut down to make way for homes and businesses, or to clear land for agriculture or mining. On roads, an estimated 4,000 wild koalas are killed each year by vehicles. Drivers are asked to pay close attention to the road when driving through a forest where wild koalas live.

There are a number of **sanctuaries** in which koalas can live safely. Lone Pine Sanctuary was created in Queensland in 1927, and koala hunting was outlawed across Australia soon after. Lone Pine was the first and largest koala sanctuary in the world. Thousands of tourists flock to the site each year, eagerly awaiting the chance to hold a koala. At the Koala Park Sanctuary in Sydney, Australia's capital city, koalas roam through man-made forests that look just like real ones.

Sometimes, the koala can actually become a little too protected, and measures must be taken to keep its numbers

In 1880, the first documented koala to leave Australia was taken to the London Zoo, where it lived for only 14 months.

Sometimes, a koala becomes too tired to continue eating and naps right where it is.

in check. Otherwise, the population can explode so much that koalas may have difficulty finding enough food or places to live. In 2005, authorities sterilized more than 8,000 koalas on Kangaroo Island in an effort to keep the population under control. Koalas had been introduced to the island in the early 20th century, but without many predators or dangers, the large population could not sustain itself on the limited natural resources available. Sterilization therefore prevented starvation for this population.

All of these efforts help ensure that the koala will be around for many more years. Australians have proven that they will not stand quietly by and watch their loveable national icon disappear, and people regularly join together in efforts to save the koala. Some even send money to the Australian Koala Foundation and become "foster parents" to koalas. Because an estimated 80 percent of koala habitat is on private land, people who live near forests are encouraged to plant eucalyptus trees. In Australia, the koala takes center stage in September, which is designated as Save the Koala Month.

The battle between saving koala habitats and human encroachment is not over, but people are determined

not to repeat the mistakes of the past that nearly resulted in the koala's extinction. The more the world knows about the plight of the koala, the better the chance that this furry animal will continue to thrive as Australia's national symbol.

The furry koala continues to endear itself to people in Australia and throughout the world.

ANIMAL TALE: THE KOALA BOY

Aborigines, the native people of Australia, have shared their continent with koalas for millennia. It could be that the gentle, peaceful nature of the koala inspired Aborigines to use koala stories to teach important life lessons. The story of the "koala boy" teaches why this animal must always be treated with respect.

Once there was a boy in Australia who lived with an aunt and uncle because his own parents had died. His aunt and uncle treated him very poorly. Even when he cried out from thirst, they gave him barely enough water to survive. He sucked on eucalyptus leaves for their water instead.

One day, the aunt and uncle left the boy alone, as they frequently did, to hunt in the dense forest. But unlike other times they had gone hunting, this time they forgot to hide the water containers. The boy greedily drank from one container and decided to hide the rest of the water high up in a tree to save for another day. He climbed a eucalyptus tree and started to sing. As he sang, the tree grew higher and higher. He was still high in the branches when his aunt and uncle arrived home. They noticed their water and the boy were missing and started to search frantically.

"Look," the aunt finally said. "The boy is high up in the tree, and he took all the water with him!"

They became very angry, but they could see that their loud voices frightened the boy.

They decided to try to coax him down with sweet words.

"Oh, little boy, please come down from the tree!" they pleaded. "We promise not to hurt you. We promise to be kind to you from now on, and we'll give you all the water you want!"

The boy was skeptical, but finally he believed them. He scurried down the tree. Once he got to the ground, his aunt and uncle became angry. He realized that he had been tricked, and they beat him badly with sticks and rocks.

But soon, a strange thing started to happen. The boy became shorter, stockier, and covered with gray fur. He became a koala! With his fast, powerful legs, he hurried back up the tree to his water vessels. The aunt and uncle shook the branches, and when that failed to bring the koala boy down, the uncle got an ax and started to chop down the tree. It worked, and the tree crashed to the ground. But when the tree fell, all the water in the containers also spilled. The water flowed away in a raging creek but soon dried up. As for the koala boy, he disappeared and was never seen again.

Since that time, the Aborigines have always been careful not to break a koala's bones nor skin it when they eat its meat. If they do so, they fear that once again, all the water in the land will spill and dry up, leaving their crops to fail in the dry and barren countryside.

GLOSSARY

antibacterial – having properties that allow for the destruction of harmful bacteria

canines – teeth at the front of the mouth that are longer than other teeth and resemble fangs

deforestation – the removal of a forest through cutting, clearing, or burning to make room for settlement and agricultural land, or harvesting trees for their natural resources

digits – the ends of the hands or feet, otherwise known as fingers, thumbs, and toes

encroach – to intrude gradually into the space of another; going beyond prescribed boundaries

goannas – large monitor lizards that are native to Australia

icon – an image that becomes associated with one subject

incisors – the front teeth that are used to cut through food

joey – the name given to some baby marsupials, including koalas and kangaroos

molars – the teeth at the back of the mouth with a wide, flat surface that are used to grind food

outback – the remote, dry, thinly populated interior regions of Australia

poachers – people who hunt protected species of wild game and fish, even though doing so is against the law

sanctuaries – places that have been set aside for refuge and protection

tufts – extensions of feathers or hair that usually form a ridge or fluffy ball

SELECTED BIBLIOGRAPHY

Defenders of Wildlife. "Koala." Kid's Planet. http://www.kidsplanet.org/factsheets/koala.html.

George, Linda. *The Koalas of Australia*. Mankato, Minn.: Bridgestone Books, 1998.

Green, Carl R., and William R. Sanford. *The Koala*. Mankato, Minn.: Crestwood House, 1987.

Hunter, Simon. *The Official Koala Handbook*. London: Chatto & Windus Limited, 1987.

Lang, Aubrey. *Baby Koala*. Allston, Mass.: Fitzhenry and Whiteside, 2004.

National Geographic Society. "Creature Feature: Koalas." National Geographic Kids. http://www.nationalgeographic.com/kids/creature_feature/0008/koalas.html.

The larger ancestors of koalas lived in Australian rainforests (pictured) millions of years ago.

INDEX